GET READY FOR GRADE 2

Daniel Shen

Spelling

Penny Dowdy

QEB

QEB Publishing

Understand...
CVC and CVCe

Editor: Amanda Askew
Designer: Red Paper Design
Illustrator: Becky Blake

Copyright © QEB Publishing, Inc. 2010

Published in the United States by
QEB Publishing, Inc.
3 Wrigley, Suite A
Irvine, CA 92618

www.qed-publishing.co.uk

A CIP record for this book is available
from the Library of Congress.

ISBN 978 1 59566 842 4

Printed in the United States by Worzalla

This book talks about CVC and CVCe.

CVC means a word made up of a consonant, a vowel, and then another consonant.

CVC	Not CVC
pin	pie
ton	toe
cut	cue

CVCe means a word made up of a consonant, a vowel, another consonant, and then the letter e. This changes the sound of the word.

CVC	CVCe
pin	pine
ton	tone
cut	cute

Contents

Short Vowels

Many words have a short vowel sound.
When you hear a word with a short vowel
sound, it may have a CVC pattern. CVC means
consonant-vowel-consonant.

Short a sound

rag

Short e sound

bed

Short i sound

pig

Short o sound

fox

Short u sound

mud

Write the words in the correct column, showing their sound. Then underline the consonants in blue and circle the vowels in red.

man	log	beg	wig	fun
red	top	run	hop	win
cap	leg	bed	dog	fig
gap	sun	rat	pin	hut

Short a	Short e	Short i	Short o	Short u

Note: As you read with children, look for words that follow the CVC pattern.

Long a and e

The long a sound sounds just like the letter a. When you hear the long a sound, spell it one of these ways.

a+e sound	ai sound	ay sound

cake	train	tray

When you add an e to a CVC word, the middle vowel gets a long sound.

 man ⟶ mane

Match the beginning of a word with its ending sound.

r__ __ __   ay

pl__ __   ake

b__ __ __   ain

The long e sound sounds just like the letter e. When you hear the long e sound, spell it one of these ways.

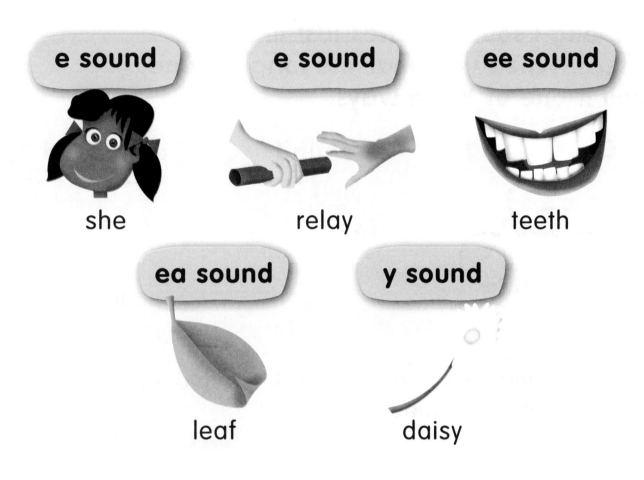

e sound

she

e sound

relay

ee sound

teeth

ea sound

leaf

y sound

daisy

Add a long e sound to each of the following words.

luck__   m__   gr__ __ n

s__ __ l   w__   w__ __ d

Note: Children may be familiar with the phrase "silent e"—the e in the CVCe pattern.

Long i, o, and U

The long i sound sounds just like the letter i. When you hear the long i sound, spell it one of these ways.

CVCe sound

y sound

igh sound

bike

sky

light

When you add an e to a CVC word, the middle vowel gets a long sound.

kit ⟶ kite

CVCe sound

The long u sound sounds just like the letter u. When you hear the long u sound, spell it like this.

mule

The long o sound sounds just like the letter o. When you hear the long o sound, spell it in one of these ways.

home

o sound

no

oa sound

boat

ow sound

snow

Find the words in the wordsearch.

bike
sky
light
home
no
boat
snow
mule

z	a	v	f	i	s	k	y
e	b	o	a	t	u	a	x
y	f	l	y	v	l	s	l
k	m	n	v	c	i	n	n
b	i	k	e	e	g	o	i
t	y	u	s	d	h	w	g
k	m	u	l	e	t	j	h
h	o	m	e	a	u	n	t
q	e	u	h	l	k	o	m

Note: Help children remember that a long vowel sound says the vowel's name.

Oo and OW Sounds

Vowels can work in teams to make different sounds. When you hear words with these sounds, spell them with these vowel teams.

oo sound

spoon

ow sound

cow

ou sound

mouse

Read the meanings. Write the correct word from the word bank.

1. A small rodent: ___ ___ ___ ___ ___

2. The beginning of a question: ___ ___ ___

3. Lights up the night: ___ ___ ___ ___

4. Another name for dog: ___ ___ ___ ___ ___ ___

5. Immediately: ___ ___ ___

now
hound
moon
how
mouse

Write a short story using oo and ow sounds. It could be about a mouse in a house, a cow on the moon, or a groom who needs a spoon.

_____

_____

_____

_____

_____

_____

_____

_____

_____

_____

Note: Children can use other words with the ow and oo sounds in their stories.

Aw Sounds

Letters can work in teams to make different sounds.

When you hear words with these sounds, spell them with these vowel teams.

aw sound	all sound

saw	ball

Add "aw" or "all" to spell the words.

c__ __ __   m__ __ __

f__ __ __   t__ __ __

cr__ __ l   sh__ __ l

dr__ __ l   b__ __ l

h__ __ __   b__ __ __

Write the words from the activity on page 12 in alphabetical order.

Note: Have children number the words on page 12 to show the alphabetical order.

R-controlled Vowels

When the letter r follows a vowel, it changes the sound the vowel makes.

These are called r-controlled vowels. Say the words aloud so you can hear how the vowel changes.

ar sound

car

er sound

waterfall

ir sound

fir

or sound

porch

ur sound

turning

Draw a line to match the rhyming words.

thorn   curl

harm   more

pour   yours

swirl   far

skirt   farm

warm   shirt

wars   storm

star   corn

Note: Rs in front of a vowel do not change the way the vowel is pronounced.

15

Clusters

Consonant clusters are two or more consonants that blend together.
Each consonant makes a sound, but they blend together. When you hear these sounds, spell them like this.

br sound

brown

gl sound

glee

st sound

stamp

tr sound

train

cl sound

clover

sw sound

swan

s u n t   __ __ u n

g i n r b   __ __ i n g

p i l c   __ __ i p

p a r t   __ __ a p

k n t u r   __ __ u n k

a d l g   __ __ a d

s a s c l   __ __ a s s

a n d t s   __ __ a n d

a g r b   __ __ a g

Note: Show children how to blend three consonant sounds in a cluster.

Consonants and h

When two or more consonants are next to each other and make a sound, you call this a digraph.

Some digraphs end in h. Read these words to recognize digraph sounds and spellings.

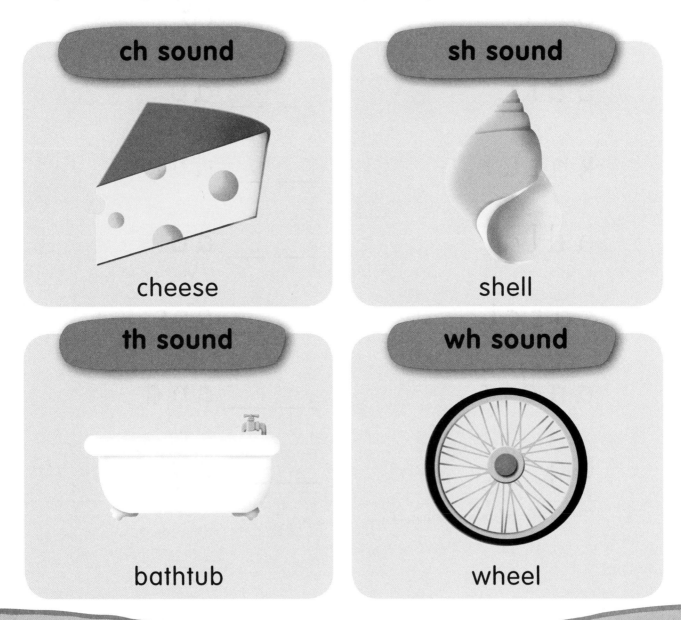

ch sound

cheese

sh sound

shell

th sound

bathtub

wh sound

wheel

Letter bank

wh	ch	sh
sh	th	wh

__ __ at   __ __ ip   __ __ ick

fi__ __   bea__ __   __ __ eat

Match your words to the words that have the same spelling pattern.

dish	__ __ at
chick	__ __ ip
pleat	__ __ ick
peach	fi__ __
that	bea__ __
clip	__ __ eat

Note: Challenge children to spell the digraphs: who, what, where, when, and why.

19

Hard and Soft c

The letter c has two different sounds.
Hard c sounds like a k. Soft c sounds like an s.
The letter k only makes the hard c sound. If you
hear words with c sounds, spell them like this.

c sound

cake

k sound

fork

ck sound

kick

s sound

city

Circle the correct word to complete each sentence.

1. A ___ is round.

   circle
   square

2. I like ___ because they are orange.

   carrots
   apples

3. I will be right ___.

   now
   back

4. I just want one ___ of pizza.

   portion
   slice

5. I ___ swim the length of the pool.

   can
   am

6. Jen stayed home because she was feeling ___.

   sick
   healthy

Now, underline the choices above that have a hard c sound.

Note: Ask children to memorize words with hard and soft c sounds.

Hard and Soft g

The letter g has two different sounds. Neither sound is like another letter. If you hear words with g sounds, spell them like this.

hard g sound

goat

soft g sound

gym

What letter makes the same sound as a soft g? Write the letter in the box below. Write two words that start with that letter, too.

Sort the spelling words into two columns, one for hard g sounds and one for soft g sounds.

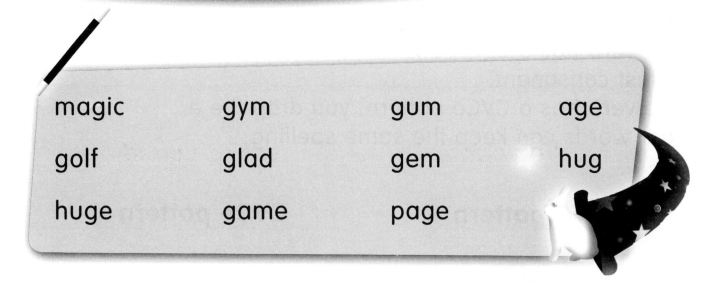

magic	gym	gum	age
golf	glad	gem	hug
huge	game	page	

hard g	soft g

Adding **ing**

Sometimes you add ing to a verb.
If the verb has a CVC pattern, you double the last consonant.
If the verb has a CVCe pattern, you drop the e.
Other words can keep the same spelling.

CVC pattern

hop ⟶ hopping

CVCe pattern

ride ⟶ riding

Other words

jump ⟶ jumping

bake   _ _ _ _ _ _ _ _

kick   _ _ _ _ _ _ _ _

stop   _ _ _ _ _ _ _ _ _

run   _ _ _ _ _ _ _ _

Think of other words that rhyme with the ing words above. Write them here.

_____

_____

_____

_____

_____

_____

Note: The ing version of a verb shows that the activity is happening right now.

Adding **ed**

Verbs have ed at the end to show they have already happened.

If the verb has a CVC pattern, you double the last consonant.

If the verb has a CVCe pattern, you drop the e.

If the word ends in y you change it to i.

Other words can keep the same spelling.

CVC pattern

sip ⟶ sipped

y ending

fry ⟶ fried

CVCe pattern

hike ⟶ hiked

Other words

camp ⟶ camped

There are 10 misspelled words below. Circle them.

"Ouch!" Sam's little sister cryed. Sam lookked over and saw she had fallen over. He skatted over to her. "Are you okay?" He askked.
"I tryed to skate over that ramp," she said as she cried.
"But I got scareed and stoped! Then I rolled off!"
Sam dryed her tears. "You rolled off?" he asked. "Like an egg?" he jokeed.
His sister laughed a little. "Yeah, kind of." Then she poped back up. "Thanks, Sam."

Spell the ed form of each verb.

Word	ed form
dine	__ __ __ __ __
study	__ __ __ __ __ __ __
net	__ __ __ __ __ __
deny	__ __ __ __ __ __
jump	__ __ __ __ __ __
bike	__ __ __ __
tip	__ __ __ __ __ __

Note: Explain that action words that end in ed are called past tense.

Adding **S** and **es**

Plural means more than one.
To spell a plural word, you add s to the end of it.
If it ends in s or a digraph, you add es.

any ending

shoe ⟶ shoes

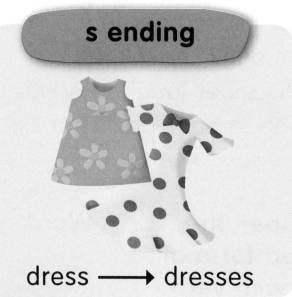

s ending

dress ⟶ dresses

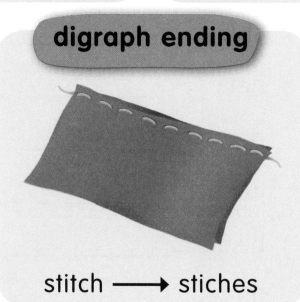

digraph ending

stitch ⟶ stiches

Make the words below into plurals.

Singular	Plural
fork	__ __ __ __ __
house	__ __ __ __ __ __
peach	__ __ __ __ __ __ __
mess	__ __ __ __ __ __
plum	__ __ __ __ __
dish	__ __ __ __ __
glass	__ __ __ __ __ __
tool	__ __ __ __ __

Look around the room. Write the plural of three things you see.

Note: Talk about words that have unusual plurals, such as oxen, knives, and fish.

29

Misspelled Words

Some words sound the same, but are spelled differently.
The best way to learn how to spell them is to memorize what each means.

Word	Meaning	Example
to	toward for	I went to her house. The letter said "To Sandy."
too	also	I like candy, too!
two	number after one	Joe has two cats.
it	object	She looked at the bag and hit it as hard as she could.
its	shows possession	The dog chewed its bone.
It's	contraction for it is	It's time to go to school.

wear	to put on	Susie didn't know what to wear!
where	what place	Where did you say you live?
we're	contraction for we are	We're going to be a little late today.
your	shows possession for you	Your mom called.
you're	contraction for you are	You're becoming a great runner!

For each sentence, choose the correct spelling.

1. ___ ___ ___ a shame that Anne didn't win.

It   Its   It's

2. Sean is coming, ___ ___ ___ .

to   too   two

3. ___ ___ ___ ___ going ___ ___ ___ ___ ___ the fun is!

we're/where
wear/where
wear/we're

4. ___ ___ ___ ___ sneakers make it seem like ___ ___ ___ ___ ___ moving so fast.

you're/your
your/you're
your/your

Note: Make flashcards with each of the commonly misspelled words.

Notes for Parents and Teachers

- Children can practice spelling with unusual materials, such as shaving cream, sand, or arts-and-crafts materials.
- Let children create a personal dictionary of words they have difficulty spelling. Children can then refer to a dictionary as needed.
- Use self-adhesive note papers to put names on common items at home.
- Teach children words that have the same spelling pattern together, such as other, brother, and mother.
- Show children how to listen for the order of sounds in a word.
- Have children break words into syllables in order to hear smaller groups of sounds.

- Do not worry if children write letters backward. This is very normal for young students. Teach them tricks for remembering directions, but avoid scolding.
- Help children write out their spelling words with colored glue onto notecards. When the glue has dried, have them trace over the letters with their fingers while spelling the words aloud.
- Create clapping chants to accompany each spelling word. The rhythm of the chant will remind children how many letters to use and help them remember the spellings.